HOW TO HEAL AND BE HAPPY AFTER SEPARATION

The
Mindful
Divorce

JAMES BRIEN

AUTHENTIC
CREATIVITY

ISBN: 978-1-9161418-1-0

First Published in 2020

As part of this product, we have created a workbook to accompany the exercises in this book. To download your FREE copy, go to:

www.themindfuldivorcebook.com

To Phoebe and Rafe - Shoot for the moon.
Even if you miss you will land among the stars.

Table of Contents

Welcome...i

Introduction..1

Dealing with Stress 6

Working Out What Went Wrong...................................14

Gratitude – Your Secret Weapon 21

Planning Your Future 27

Coping in a Crisis..40

Summary..51

Appendix..55

Acknowledgements 56

Welcome

When I got divorced, I found I had no one to turn to for advice. Although half of all marriages end in divorce, I could only think of one friend who had been through it at the time and he lived overseas in Spain.

Most of the advice available online was terrible. I found many divorce forums, but they were full of angry and emotional rants. That was the last thing I needed. What I wanted was clear guidance to help me navigate this uncertain time in my life.

I felt very much alone, and during the pain, I promised myself that once I got my life back in order following divorce, I would write a book to help others do the same.

Somewhat naively, I titled my first book, *The Real Man's Guide to Divorce*. A real man, in my opinion, is someone who does the right thing, for himself and his family; someone who faces up to his responsibilities. I knew the title was slightly controversial, but it was chosen to pique interest not alienate people.

Many women were involved throughout the writing process, and although it was written mainly for men, women purchased the book for family members (including the mother of my ex-wife's boyfriend - but that's another story). Feedback was resoundingly positive, which provided me with the inspiration to write this new book for men and women.

I've coached many people going through a divorce, and know that each situation is different. Some initiated the divorce and have in many ways come to terms with it. Some are on the receiving end and are still in shock or denial. Some have children, and others have complicated finances. Some are on good terms with their spouse, and some can't stand to be in the same room as them. I also realised that most people don't want to spend any more time then they need to, thinking about and dealing with divorce.

This is the first in a series of short, concise books aimed at giving you the information you need to make the right decisions and choices around your divorce. I want to show you how to avoid any negative consequences that can happen when couples separate permanently. I've focused in on specific topics that, once addressed, can help you lead a healthy, positive and happy life – even if right at this moment, you don't see that as a possibility.

This book is focused primarily on our mental resilience because, as I will show you, this is the most critical factor in helping you successfully negotiate the challenges of divorce.

What makes this book even more pertinent is that it publishes in the middle of a global pandemic, the likes of which we have not seen in a hundred years. Separation and divorce are hard enough, but the social and economic challenges of the Covid-19 crisis create significant additional problems. And even the lockdown itself is likely to create a spike in divorce rates. There are many couples who are only able to stay together because they spend a lot of time apart. Forced together, personal tensions are magnified which can lead some to re-evaluate their lives and what is important to them.

We are being told to avoid any unnecessary contact. For most of us, that means no office, no school, no travel, no restaurants, no gym and no group activities. Instead we must stay at home as much as possible. At the time of writing, we don't know how long this will go on for, but we do know that restrictions will be lifted slowly, and it will take many months for our lives to return to normal.

Depending on your current situation, you may find yourself tied to a spouse or partner that you don't want to be with anymore. Or, perhaps worse, you are isolated on your own, away from friends, and even your children. It's situations like these that can heighten your emotions and possibly lead you to finding yourself in extreme or unimaginable scenarios. Escaping by binge watching TV or obsessively browsing the internet will only increase your anxiety as you are bombarded by extreme negativity and scaremongering.

When we are on edge and in a state of high anxiety, we can't think straight. We make bad decisions and do things or ignore things that can have a negative long-term effect on our health, wealth and spirit. What we need to do is to be able to put some space between ourselves and the noise going on inside of our heads.

This book will give you the tools to manage your stress levels, improve your mood and get clarity on what you want from your life so that you know how to move forward. When we don't know what we want, our environment drives us, pushing us one way or another. We lose control. When we know exactly what we want from life, it doesn't matter what happens around us, we roll with the challenges, adjust our course and continue towards our goals.

I want to show you how to make the very best of this situation. I will show you how to come through it stronger, happier and healthier. It might seem impossible to you right now, but I know from my own and my client's experiences, that you will feel better if you follow the processes in this book. You owe it to yourself and your family, to be in the best possible position to deal with the challenges ahead.

I hope you find this book helpful and that you put the techniques to good use. Let me know your comments, feedback and success stories at james@themindfuldivorcebook.com. With your permission, I will use them in later editions of the book to benefit other readers.

To meet like-minded people, you can join our community, The Mindful Divorce Club, on Facebook.

Introduction

S eparation is the end of a relationship between two people. Regardless of who initiated it, who wants it and who doesn't, or whether it was a mutual decision, it hurts. However, the way you handle yourself post-split will be the key to your recovery.

The flood of emotions and feelings that you will experience is unlike anything else. These feelings will rush in and out and vary in intensity. You may feel despair, anger, sadness, a sense of being lost or a lack of motivation. You may feel a physical ache in your stomach that will not subside. You may feel extremely sensitive, and everything may remind you of your spouse. All of these feelings are natural, but this doesn't provide much comfort when you are going through what may be the hardest time in your life.

But there is good news. All of these feelings will subside over time and eventually go away. The keyword here is time, but you can also be proactive to facilitate the healing process. If you start on a dark path of self-destruction, however, it will only take more time to heal, and you will hurt for longer than necessary.

It is understandable to want to numb the pain and perhaps drink in excess. However - as you may have already experienced - alcohol is a depressant; it will bring your mood down. Everything will feel worse, especially when the hangover kicks in. Then you start beating yourself: Is it just me? Will I ever find anyone again? Am I destined to a life of misery? To avoid entering this negative spiral, steer clear of alcohol and other drugs.

So what can you do to start the healing process? Well, first, we should acknowledge the elephant in the room. Healing and moving forward to a life of happiness, requires you to do things that you may not feel like doing. Some days you may feel like not doing anything at all and that's ok. Sometimes it's better to be kind to yourself and give yourself a break so that you can come back stronger and fight another day.

Some recommendations, like getting out of the house for a walk or jog, will be easy for some, but could be more challenging for a parent with younger children for example. But they are so effective, it is worth committing to, even if this means, arranging childcare or bringing the children with you. Exercise causes your body to release endorphins, and these feel-good chemicals raise your mood and put you in a more resourceful state of mind. You can use this resourceful state to help you take on other tasks that require more mental effort, such as talking to friends and family.

I vividly remember the internal battles I used to have about reaching out to friends during the early stages of my separation. I would talk myself out of picking up the phone, thinking that I had to lift myself out of my mental fug first, not realising that picking up the phone and hearing a friendly voice would instantly lift my spirits.

I thought that it was my responsibility to sort myself out, and it wasn't fair to burden my friends with my problems. But the truth was that my friends and your friends too would be so disappointed if we didn't reach out to them.

Thinking about it for a second; if your best friend was suffering and they didn't come to you for help, how would you feel? Disappointed? Hurt? Maybe even angry? These would be understandable reactions because we want to help our friends and those around us. It is an inherent nature in us all.

So reach out and don't isolate yourself. Surround yourself with people who love and care about you, people who will build you up and support you. Being alone, overthinking and reminiscing achieves nothing. Set yourself small daily challenges to pick up the phone or try a Zoom call. One of the benefits of lockdown is that everyone is at home and desperate to talk with someone. You will see that the simple act of talking with a friend, releases tension and helps you see your situation more clearly.

While we need people in our lives to help lift our spirits, beware of falling into the trap of flirting with old flames or getting into new relationships. Even if you think of it as a bit of harmless fun, that isn't going to go anywhere. Yes, it can feel good, and it takes your mind off your situation. But you run the risk of rebounding and getting into a new relationship prematurely, creating even more inner conflict.

While our goal is to get over the heartbreak and move on, for long term happiness and wellbeing we need to give ourselves the space to deal with our emotions rather than distracting ourselves with new relationships. It is also important to identify any mistakes that we made in our previous relationship to avoid making the same mistake twice.

Undoubtedly this will hurt, feeling some pain is unavoidable, but pain is not something that we should continually run from or shut out. Nor is it something that we should hold on to and embrace. Pain usually teaches us something, so recognise your pain, learn from it and let it go.

Know that the pain that you are feeling will dwindle and ultimately go away, but this process does take time. My hope for you is that you use this time to develop yourself and build up your confidence and by following this series of books you will learn to take care of yourself and start living the life that *you* want to live.

This book is packed with techniques to help you manage your stress, come to terms with your situation, feel happier and more optimistic while planning for a brighter future. As you start working through the exercises, you will find that as your confidence rises, your pain will subside. With higher confidence, everything gets better. You will be in a better place emotionally, and you will attract beautiful experiences and people into your life.

There is no escaping from the fact that separation hurts. But if you set yourself up for failure by pressing the self-destruct button, the pain will increase and last much longer than necessary. By taking care of yourself, developing your confidence and enhancing your self-worth, you will bounce back more quickly. This is how you can successfully navigate divorce.

The tools and techniques in this book will help you in the short term but also and importantly, support you in your future life. I hope that you will look back on this time and recognise it as a turning point, a pivotal time when you learned how to lead a happier life and develop and nurture better relationships.

Dealing with Stress

"The greatest weapon against stress is our ability to choose one thought over another."

William James

T he specifics of each divorce are unique, but we all tend to go through a similar set of emotions. Understandably, many people experience a deep sense of loneliness. You will likely replay scenarios and decisions over and over in your head.

You might ask yourself: What if I had done things differently? Would that have saved the marriage? Am I doing the right thing? Is there anything else I can do?

You will feel anger and, of course, sadness. Thinking about special days such as birthdays and Christmas can increase the intensity of such emotions, especially if children are involved.

Despite this, you must remember that these feelings are normal. It is a process, an emotional rollercoaster that will eventually stop. For now, while you are on the ride, the best you can do is keep calm and take care of yourself.

It is essential to look after yourself physically and mentally during this process, so we will start by looking at how you can manage stress, because, as we will see, the way in which you cope with it will have a significant impact on your overall wellbeing.

What is Stress?

We've all felt it, but what exactly is stress? At the most basic level, stress is our body's reaction to pressures from a situation or life event. Despite its reputation, stress is a normal part of life and not necessarily a bad thing.

When stressed, the oldest part of our brain responsible for our survival, thinks we are under attack and sends out signals to release hormones to prepare us to either fight or run away. This kept our ancestors alive by alerting them to potential danger, such as a sabre-toothed tiger.

In the modern world, the fight or flight response can still help us survive dangerous situations, such as quickly slamming on the brakes when someone runs in front of our car; thankfully these incidents occur infrequently. Instead, we experience relatively minor stressors all of the time, but left unchecked, these can build up and put our bodies into a permanent state of stress, that can cause us to react with an excessive response to a situation.

When we are in a state of stress, blood flow is diverted to the most important muscles needed to fight or flee and brain function is minimised, meaning we literally cannot think straight. Instead, we may feel agitated and aggressive towards others which can negatively affect relationships and ruin reputations.

When a person faces continuous challenges without relief, the fight or flight response can become chronically activated, causing physical and emotional wear and tear on the body. This can lead to a medical condition called distress, a negative stress reaction.

Distress can disturb the body's internal balance, leading to physical symptoms such as headaches, an upset stomach, elevated blood pressure, chest pain, sexual dysfunction, and problems sleeping. Emotional problems can include depression, panic attacks, or other forms of anxiety and worry.

Research suggests that stress also can bring on or worsen certain symptoms or diseases and is linked to six of the leading causes of death: heart disease, cancer, lung ailments, accidents, cirrhosis of the liver, and suicide.

Stress also becomes harmful when people engage in the compulsive use of substances or behaviours to try to relieve their stress, such as food, alcohol, sex and shopping. Rather than reducing the stress and returning the body to a relaxed state, these substances and compulsive behaviours tend to keep the body in a stressed state and cause more problems, thus the distressed person becomes trapped in a vicious circle.

Coping Strategies for Managing Stress

What contributes to stress can vary dramatically from person to person and differs according to our social and economic circumstances, the environment we live in and our experience of dealing with it. Characteristic of the things that can make us feel stress include experiencing something new or unexpected, something that threatens our feeling of self, or feeling that we have little control over a situation.

Divorce, by its very nature, is a stressful situation. It is often a new situation and may be unexpected. Most of our identity will be tied up with our status of being married as a wife or a husband, and you may be worried about how divorce will impact your role as a mother or a father. Divorce has a way of making us think we don't have control, which is not the case. You will find that the things you can control, such as finding resources to help you through this time, educating yourself on the process, and asking for guidance and support when you need it, will far outnumber the things that you cannot control.

To get you started it's helpful to understand that there are three basic coping strategies for managing stress:

- Solution-Focused: Doing something to manage or change a situation
- Emotion-Focused: Managing your emotional response to a situation rather than changing the situation
- Avoidance-Focused: Ignoring or refusing to accept a situation or distracting yourself from it

The avoidance style is not helpful and could lead to further problems, especially when using alcohol as a distraction. If you are faced with a situation that you can change, a solution-focused approach will likely work best. However, if you are dealing with a situation that is out of your control, an emotion-focused response will be your best option.

During a divorce, as in life, some things are controllable, and some things are not. For example, you have little control over your ex-partner's behaviour. But, you have full control of how you react to him or her, and you can use the emotion-focused approach successfully so that his or her actions do not negatively affect your mood.

Of course, interrupting your primitive brain's propensity to go ballistic when your spouse is difficult and serenely managing your emotional response isn't easy, but it is possible. It is a learned behaviour; the more you practice, the easier it becomes until it becomes your default setting.

What makes this process easier, is reducing the overall amount of stress in your life, as the more stressed you become, the less effective you will be in handling tasks and emotions.

But what if stress has built to the point where it's affecting your ability to function? This is called overwhelm, which is our body's way of telling us that we have too much going on in our heads and we have to find a way to deal with it. You can do this by following these simple steps.

Step 1. Get the thoughts out of your head and write them down

Produce a list of everything that you must do, or that is worrying you. Once your concerns are on paper, they each become a tangible item to tackle.

Step 2. Prioritise

Work through your list and decide what the most important things to deal with are. You cannot do everything at once. In this process, you will only address one thing at a time, so you must prioritise your list.

Don't get too hung up on the list itself. If anything needs changing, amend it later. You will likely have several minor things that are bothering you, but when you consider them against the others, you will find that they are low in priority. This process helps to eliminate this noise. Trust the process.

Step 3. Relax and smile for at least two minutes

I know this sounds ludicrous, and it is probably the last thing you want to do, but there is science behind this approach. The physiological movement of smiling releases chemicals in our bodies called endorphins, which help us feel happier. So, think of something that makes you smile, your children, a funny friend, and relax and take some deep breaths.

Step 4. Schedule the first thing on your list

In other words, decide when you will begin or complete your first task. The aim is to schedule it for today or tomorrow, at the latest.

Step 5. Take action

Taking action does not necessarily mean completing the full task at once, as it might contain multiple steps, but you must do something to move towards completion.

Perhaps you are worried about money, and how you are going to support yourself and your children? A starting point could be to list the resources that can provide you with more information, such as the Citizens Advice Bureau, an online child maintenance calculator, or a divorce coach. Next, choose which action to complete first, for instance, sending an email to schedule an appointment. By completing this task, you are taking a definitive step towards your overall goal.

Step 6. Celebrate

Every time you accomplish something, cross it off your list and celebrate. Celebrating has a beneficial effect: it trains the mind. The mind likes to feel reward, so celebrating every accomplishment teaches it to expect a reward after completing a task. Soon, your mind begins to move in the direction of finding solutions to problems because it knows it will receive a reward. This process is simple, but it works. Aim to write your list each week. Writing will take longer at first, but once you have completed the exercise a few times, it will become second nature.

Other Ways to Reduce Stress

Coping with stress is not always about doing. Sometimes we need to give ourselves a break and allow ourselves some downtime to take our mind off our problems. Here are some other ways to reduce the feeling of stress:

Seek out social support and spend enough time with those who care for you and support you.

Find something that you enjoy. Perhaps this activity is something that you used to do but don't anymore or something new that you have always wanted to try.

Learn how to relax properly. Try yoga or meditation. Both have an incredible effect on your body. There are numerous meditation apps available, but I recommend *10 Percent Happier* because it also explains how meditation works.

Make sure you are getting enough sleep. Go to bed at a time that allows you to get up early. Establish and maintain a routine. Win the morning, and you win the day.

Eat a balanced diet, and make sure to exercise. Remember junk in, junk out. If you want to feel good and tackle anything that life throws at you, then fuel and train your body like the incredible machine that it is. Exercise has the additional benefit of reducing stress instantly.

Keep a positive attitude and maintain a sense of humour. Laughter is scientifically proven to really be the best medicine, so aim to see the fun in life. Chat with friends or watch stand-up or comedy shows. Not only will laughter make you feel better, but it also boosts your immune system.

Don't suffer in silence, if you are finding it challenging to manage your stress levels, talk to a friend or join our facebook community.

Working Out What Went Wrong

"Divorce isn't such a tragedy. A tragedy's staying in an unhappy marriage, teaching your children the wrong things about love."

Jennifer Weiner

S eparating can make you feel like a failure, in a world where we tend to try to avoid failing at all costs. We're so focused on not failing that we settle for a life of mediocrity, ignoring warning signs and glossing over the severity of our situation.

But isn't the real failure staying in a loveless relationship? Would you rather spend 50 years in an unfulfilling relationship or admit that you messed up? Wouldn't it be better to learn from your experience, and then spend the next 50 years living a happy and fulfilling life? That's what we will do next. We are going to get clarity on what went wrong. This requires you to have an open mind and to take personal responsibility for your part in the breakup.

There are seven primary reasons why couples separate; infidelity; substance abuse; lack of commitment; excessive conflict; growing apart; financial problems; and getting married too young. Which category resonates with you?

Who initiated your separation? Was it you, was it your partner, or was it a mutual decision? If we take infidelity as an example, and you were the offender, consider why you were unfaithful. The purpose isn't to beat yourself up. The goal is to learn from it so that it doesn't happen again.

Maybe you feel like you just can't stay with one partner. If that's the case, that's fine, but don't enter into another serious relationship without being honest and open from the start. Maybe you got drunk, and you cheated. Perhaps the lesson here is to know your limits and not put yourself in that situation again.

What if your ex-partner cheated on you? Don't be a victim as that won't help you. Think about what you can learn from this instead. Is there some way that you could have contributed to the situation? Were you pushing him or her away? Were they just the wrong person for you? If so, what are the personality traits or the early warning signs that you can now recognise in future partners?

Lack of commitment, too much conflict, growing apart, and separating because you married too young all boil down to the same thing: conflicting values. What are values? Well, it's probably easier, to begin with, what values are not.

Values are not about which Netflix shows you like or what type of music you enjoy. Values are your personal, individual beliefs about what is most important to you. They represent your belief system about what is right and wrong, good and bad.

We need values to move forward in life. Without them, we won't feel whole and fulfilled but, rather, empty. We feel deep personal satisfaction when our behaviour fulfils our values. This concept is called congruity.

Values govern our lives and how we respond to any given situation. They are like the human equivalent of iOS or Android. Every app, or experience, is affected by the operating system.

So where do we get our values? Values are specific, highly emotional beliefs that come from the environment in which we were raised. Our mothers and fathers, our role models, tell us what to do and what not to do. We receive a reward if we accept their guidelines and punishment if we do not. This punish-reward technique programmes most of the values that we carry. As we age, we also begin to internalise values from our teachers, friends and cultural icons such as sports and movie stars.

It is essential to understand our values so that we can choose the proper behaviours to support them. So how do we discover our values? We can ask ourselves a series of simple questions. For example, let's say that you want to find out what you value in an intimate relationship. You can begin by asking yourself: What is important to me in a close relationship, and why?

Let's say that love was your first answer. You would then ask yourself: What is important about love in a personal relationship? With each answer, ask the same question again until you feel that you have exhausted your list. Write your answers down on a piece of paper. You should have a list that looks like this:

Love	Openness	Acceptance
Happiness	Honesty	Appreciation
Compatibility	Commitment	Fun
Respect	Understanding	Beauty

Now that you have your list, you need to prioritise the entries. Duplicate your entries along the top of your page like the example below. Start on the first row, in this case 'happiness' and ask yourself if 'happiness' is more important than the value in each column, in this example 'love'. If it is more important, mark it with an 'x' and move on to the next column and ask yourself if happiness is more important than 'respect', each time marking 'x' if it is more important. Once you've completed each column, move down to the next row, 'love' and follow the same process.

	Happiness	Love	Respect	Honesty	Trust	
Happiness		x				1
Love						0
Respect	x	x				2
Honesty	x	x	x			3
Trust	x	x	x	x		4

After you complete the exercise, total up the scores for each value. The values with the highest scores are your most meaningful values, so you can now ensure that future relationships align with these beliefs.

Although we are focusing on relationships, it is essential to recognise that the conflicts you have with your partner are not always about the relationship itself. A conflict arises when two people disagree with each other. A common source of disagreement in many relationships is money.

In this case, understanding your attitude and values around money can help you avoid discord in your relationship. Imagine, for example, that you believe in respecting money and using it wisely. If your partner doesn't appreciate money in the same way and prefers to spend it all, this disparity in values will create friction and tension within your relationship.

For this reason, it is essential to examine your values in several different aspects of your life. Quite often, people say that opposites attract. After all, contrasting personalities can certainly add intensity and excitement to a new relationship, and conflicts can generate sparks and sexual energy. However, the relationship will eventually sour.

If respect is important to you, but your partner tends to badmouth or belittle you, the disparity will create cracks in your relationship. Maybe honesty is vital to your partner, but you have a habit of telling little white lies. Or perhaps being adventurous is crucial to you, but your partner is more reserved.

Sometimes when we meet someone, the intensity of the relationship can obscure the difference in values. As the excitement settles down, cracks begin to form. You suddenly start to get annoyed by things that you never noticed before.

Various peer groups form our values as we move through life. So as we grow older, our values and attributes can change. We sometimes find that we have less in common and don't want the same as our partner anymore. When we have different values from our partner, we might behave in a way that's incongruent with our values, or we might impose our values on our partner. In either case, one or both parties may feel frustrated or conflicted.

The problem is that values are so deep-seated and carry so much emotion that they're hard to identify. We may just feel some level of unease or discomfort. Sometimes, this small amount of pain can build over time and break the relationship. At other times, the pain is extremely powerful and causes immediate friction and conflict.

Now that you understand the importance of values, stop reading and complete the exercise described earlier. Go through every important element of your life; your relationships; your career; your work; your finances; your children; and ask yourself those questions to prioritise your values.

Once you have ranked your list, look through it to see if anything jumps out at you as a conflict that you had with your ex-partner. My problem arose once I had children, and they became my number one priority. After coming home from work, I would give all of my attention to my daughter. I didn't think I was doing anything wrong, and I felt that my ex-wife would understand my behaviour. However, I didn't realise that I was hurting her feelings. She no longer felt loved. Instead, she felt like she was second best.

I learned that I need to be more balanced and less extreme in relationships, which admittedly is difficult for me. I need to make sure that I make time for both my partner and my children, as they are both deserving of my love and attention.

The realisations that you gain from this process can be incredibly powerful. This process involves being accountable for your actions instead of blaming somebody else. Identifying the part that I'd played in the breakup of my marriage and holding myself accountable made me feel good. It made me feel like I was acting in line with my values, that I was being responsible.

I felt so much better because I knew that I'd discovered a valuable lesson. When you learn, you grow, and when you grow, you feel alive. Even though your divorce was not a life goal, you will become a stronger person if you learn from it.

Gratitude – Your Secret Weapon

"Piglet noticed that even though he had a Very Small Heart, it could hold a rather large amount of Gratitude."

A.A. Milne

I t is quite likely that you are not at your peak at the moment. You might feel down or find that your mood swings through emotions such as anger, regret and guilt. I'm going to give you a simple exercise that will help you feel considerably better about yourself and your future.

Holding on to negative thoughts can be extremely damaging to your health. The basis of this exercise is the principle that you cannot hold on to a negative emotion if you feel gratitude towards something else.

Depending on your current circumstances, finding things to be grateful for might be difficult, but if you stick with the process, I promise that you will feel better about yourself.

Get a pen and notebook for this exercise. For it to be effective, you must write down your answers. Just thinking about them in your head won't work, as your brain will merge all of your other ideas, resulting in a vague notion at best. When you write a thought down, it becomes more real and tangible. It is no longer just a thought.

You can also use technology such as a phone, tablet or computer, but the physical act of writing is preferable because linking the mind and body unlocks our subconscious thoughts. Perform the exercise day and night for two weeks. If you keep up the practice, you will notice a continued improvement in your mood and frame of mind.

Start each morning by completing the following:

1. Set a goal for the day

Set a goal that you will complete by the end of the day, so make sure it is achievable. It can be anything. Think about the day ahead and where you might be able to push yourself out of your current comfort zone. For example, you could say hello to five strangers during a walk, call a friend for a chat, or sign up for a study class.

2. Decide what you are willing to give or do for others today

This is where reciprocity comes into play. Good things will happen to you when you give to others. So ask yourself: What am I willing to give to others today? It could be helping a colleague at work or reaching out to a friend or a family member who might be struggling right now. Your good deed doesn't have to be big, but it must be something that you do for someone else.

3.   Identify ten things that you are grateful for right now

You might find this hard at first but stick with it. List ten things that you are grateful for: your health, your children, your parents, your friends. Hell, at the moment I'm just grateful that I woke up this morning and I have Wi-Fi! Keep going and make sure that you write down at least ten.

Getting into the habit of finding things that you feel grateful for is one of the best things you can do for yourself. This practice is about focusing on what is good in our lives and being thankful for the things we have. People who often feel grateful and appreciative are happier, less stressed and less depressed. Gratitude is an antidote to the sadness and disappointment we feel when we think about what is missing from our lives.

Positive emotions are contagious: one often leads to another. When we feel grateful, we might also feel happy, calm, joyful or loving.

Gratitude can also lead to positive actions. When we feel grateful for someone's kindness towards us, we are more likely to perform an act of kindness in return. In turn, our gratitude can have a positive effect on someone else's actions.

Don't just list big things. Recognising the small things is beneficial too, as they usually happen more frequently. One morning I found myself thinking about all of the people who enabled me to buy a cup of coffee: farmers, roasters, truck drivers, paper cup makers. It is incredible to consider everything that was involved in the process of making this seemingly minor thing we often take for granted. At the time of writing with all of the coffee shops closed during a pandemic, this might seem obvious, but it's easy to take everything for granted when all is back to normal.

4. Write one thing that another person did for you

Rather than a general feeling of appreciation, this habit seeks to identify why you are grateful about a specific person. Again, it doesn't have to be a grand gesture; a chat with a friend who makes you laugh works. Just make sure the act is recent and personal to you.

5. Write one thing that you are happy about right now

You might have to dig deep, but there will be something, somewhere that can make you feel happy. I love poached eggs, so eating poached eggs for breakfast makes me happy. It feels a little like I've gone out for breakfast, that I'm having a bit of luxury. What matters is that you find something. Even feeling only a glimmer of happiness indicates that the exercise is working. Stick with the task, and it will become more natural, more genuine and more powerful as you continue the process.

And that's it. The whole process shouldn't take longer than five or ten minutes. Finish it, then go about your day.

Before bed, come back to your notebook and complete the following three tasks:

1. Review your progress towards today's goal

Look at the goal that you set for the day and write a few words on how it went. Setting goals is very beneficial. There's the benefit of actually achieving your goals, of course, but the positives go deeper than that.

Goals lead us to feel hopeful and confident. They add a sense of structure and meaning to life. When we get into the habit of setting goals and striving to achieve them, we build our confidence to reach even greater purposes. Higher confidence, in turn, strengthens our resilience and develops a deep knowing that we can overcome the challenges that life throws at us.

2. Make a note of what you did or gave to others today

In the morning, you set yourself a goal to do or give something to another person. In the evening, write a few words about what you did and the outcome, especially how it made the other person feel and how it made you feel.

Reviewing in this way reinforces constructive behaviour because you feel great when you think about your good deeds. You are also being held accountable for that goal, so you are more likely to follow through on it.

3. Write down something that made you happy

It could be something that happened to you or something that you did that you are celebrating. As you go through the process each day, you will find and document more and more good things that happened to you.

Record what happens over the next two weeks, and you will be amazed at how your feelings and your output will improve. You might want to give yourself a 'happiness' score each morning to track your progress. There is no science behind it; just score how happy you feel on a scale of 1 to 10.

What you focus on is what you receive in life. If you pay attention to negativity, you will notice more and more things that make you feel negative. On the other hand, if you direct your focus on positive things, you will experience more positivity. It's that simple. If you want more of something, show appreciation for it, and it will naturally flow towards you.

Planning Your Future

"By recording your dreams and goals on paper, you set in motion the process of becoming the person you most want to be. Put your future in good hands - your own."

Mark Victor Hansen

One of the best goal setting techniques I have ever used is called the Clarity Tool from performance coach, Dean Graziosi. It is a goal setting exercise with a difference. We can achieve so much more in life when we know the destination before we begin. Very quickly, you will see where you are (starting point), where you want to go (target) and why you want to go there (motivation).

Knowing your 'why' is particularly important because it gives you the drive needed to reach your goals when life isn't so good. Like, for example, when you are going through a divorce, and you have had another disagreement with your spouse. Or you've lost your job due to the coronavirus, and you are uncertain and perhaps fearful about your future.

Once you know your starting point and destination, and you are excited about getting there, all that stands in the way is having the skills and capabilities to achieve your goals. This is the 'how', and this is what I aim to share with you in my books.

The design of this tool will get you laser-focused on the direction you want to take in life. In our busy world, we are constantly bombarded with messages that seek to persuade us to think or act in a certain way.

Sometimes this is beneficial and even necessary in areas such as education, being active and learning new skills. More often than not, messages with shocking headlines and clickbait make us fearful, while images on social media that create FOMO (fear of missing out), jealousy and anxiety, distract us from the reality of our real world.

These messages have the ability to knock us from our path. How many times have you gone online to pay a bill or send an email only to find yourself 30 minutes later, deep down some social media rabbit hole?

We can journey down many different paths, but there are only a few things in our life that move us towards where we want to go, not to where outside influences guide us, and this is what we will look at next.

Take a piece of paper and draw a cross through the middle, so you have four sections. Write the following, one for each section:

Current status.	One year goals
Why these goals are important	Capabilities needed to achieve these goals

Defining your Current Status

To begin, you are going to write where you currently are. If we want to go somewhere, even if it is in our car, we need to know where we are so that we can plan our route.

Your starting point is crucial because all change starts with honesty. You bought this book because you want to change something. There is something or a situation in your life that you want to improve.

Maybe you're struggling with your mood. Or you are worried about money and where you are going to live. Maybe you miss your kids and don't know how you will cope, seeing them less. Or you are scared about being on your own. Whatever it is, write it down the honest, unvarnished truth.

This exercise might feel painful; in fact, it should feel painful. Get uncomfortable; no one is going to know what you write except for you. Expose the pain and put salt on it because pain creates action. Pleasure and pain are the two primary human motivations. Every decision we make and every step we take either move us away from pain or to move us towards pleasure, and pain is the more powerful of the two. You will have done more in your life to avoid pain than you have to experience pleasure.

Push yourself for the truth. Don't just say: "I'm separated from my family." Write what this means to you. Even if your current situation feels terrible, and you don't want to go there, the practice of writing it down makes it better, not worse. When we are unclear of our situation, our worries stack on top of each other, compounding our troubles and making us feel worse. Even if you don't consciously hear the thoughts, it goes on in your subconscious creating deep unease.

Left unchecked our minds run wild. American author Mark Twain famously said: "I've had a lot of worries in my life, most of which never happened." When we write our current situation down, it gives us the clarity we need to take action, which provides us with a feeling of empowerment. We feel in control; we tell ourselves that we've got this. Have you ever noticed how you always feel better, and concern disappears when you start to take action towards a problem, even if the step is small?

If I had completed this exercise five years ago when I first separated, my truth would have been that I was scared that divorce was going to mess up my kids.

I was worried that I didn't have enough money and stressed that I wouldn't be able to provide for my kids and look after myself. I was frustrated about losing many of the material things I'd worked hard to acquire. I'd unashamedly worked ridiculously long hours, often at the expense of my family, social life and health to buy a better car, a bigger house and extravagant holidays to create what I thought a dream life, and now I was going to lose at least half of it. I felt like I was back to square one. My friends still had all of their stuff, and here I was at 40 years old with literally nothing. I felt embarrassed; I felt like a failure.

I was worried that I would grow apart from my kids and that someday I wouldn't be relevant or have any significance in their lives. I was concerned about not seeing my kids enough. I felt like I'd let them down.

It bothered me that I didn't have any positive reference points. Everything I read was negative. Everyone I spoke to only had horror stories; I felt like I was treading a lonely path. It felt like what I wanted - happy kids post-divorce - was an impossibility.

I was worried that I was tarnished, that I would be considered damaged goods. I remember asking myself, who would want to go on a date with a divorcee? Just the word divorcee carried so much weight and negativity for me at the time.

I don't think of myself as a worrier, but looking back, I clearly was. I share this with you now to encourage you to do the same. Be completely honest with yourself. Take your piece of paper and give yourself at least three minutes and write down where you are right now.

The Best Year of Your Life

Next, you are going to write where you want to go, but we are going to do it a little differently. Separation is a very stressful time without also having to contend with the outcomes of the coronavirus pandemic. Being surrounded by so much chaos makes goal setting difficult because we can't see through the dust. This next step will help you get clarity on your goals because you are going to pretend it's a year from now and you have just had the best year of your life.

When you look back, what does the best year of your life look like to you? Is it a stress-free, happy life? Do you have time for yourself and time for your kids? Are you seeing friends and family, people who energise you and make you feel good? Are you enjoying regular exercise, and are you in the best shape of your life? Are you doing a job you love and making lots of money? Or have you fulfilled a lifelong ambition and set your own business up? Are you blissfully happy in a new intimate relationship?

When you write down your goals, it has to be what you want, not what you don't want. Very often when you ask someone what they want out of life, they'll tell you what they don't want. People do this because they are running on a treadmill, trying to keep up with the rest of the world. They don't have time to stop and work out what they want. Usually, they are focused on the outside world, the nagging spouse, the Machiavellian boss, the neighbour's new car. Because their focus is on outside influences, what other people want them to do, or what they think they should do based on someone else's opinion rather than their own, they feel discontentment, and so they tell you what they don't want.

I don't want to be stressed. I don't want to be nagged. I don't want to be disrespected. I don't want to feel ashamed about my car.

Can you remember when you first learned how to drive? The driving instructor would tell you to keep your distance from the parked cars ahead, and you'd start to move towards them, seemingly without even turning the wheel. Without realising it, you put your focus on the parked cars instead of taking a safe passage ahead. You tell yourself; don't hit the car, don't hit the car, all the while focusing on the car until the driver instructor takes control of the wheel and steers you both to safety.

Eventually, you learn to scan ahead in the direction of travel, aware of obstacles but not solely focused on them. It is the same with our goals; what we focus on is where we go. But when we focus on what we don't want, in our relationships, or health, or any part of our life, the result is that we get more of what we don't want.

I want this exercise to help you get to your bigger, brighter future. I want you to know where you want to go so that you can put all of your energy and focus in the right direction. When you are clear on what you want, and you have an unwavering focus on achieving it, you don't get distracted and knocked off course by external things that you can't control anyway, such as the coronavirus.

By getting clarity on where you want to go, you can point yourself in the right direction. The only way to get there is to give it all your energy, but we only have a certain amount of energy to give. So we have to be crystal clear on what we want and focus our finite energy and effort on getting there. If we don't have focus, we get swayed by external influences. We end up getting distracted and doing things that someone else wants us to do. So be clear on your goals. Fuzzy targets don't get hit.

When I did this exercise, my children lived 300 miles away in Cornwall, and I was in London. Every other weekend I would drive for 12 hours. Most weeks I would spend another ten hours on the train travelling to my office in the Lake District. And also, I had frequent international travel to the Middle East and Asia. I spent about half my time in a different bed, and I wasn't sure how I could keep this schedule up.

When I looked back on the best 12 months of my life, I came up with the following:

- All debt paid off
- Freedom to work from home
- Live in Cornwall near my children
- Have a happy and healthy relationship with my kids and my ex-wife
- Have a healthy and fit body
- Write a book to help others going through a divorce
- Contribute to the local community / set up a kids' charity
- Fill my time with people who make me feel good

Now it is your turn. What does the best year of life look like to you? Start writing it down. Give yourself at least six minutes, and when complete circle the top five or six that are most important to you. These are your goals.

Do take the time and do this. If you just read through and think that you do it later, then the chances are you won't do it. And if you don't, you are missing an opportunity to give yourself a life-changing experience.

I know that sounds strong, but if you follow through on these exercises, you will have more clarity and more vision than the majority of people on the planet. Most people go through life on autopilot. They react to the world around them. They don't realise that they have a choice.

They get distracted, manipulated, coerced into doing things, and it never occurs to them to question if this is what they want. All they feel is a sense of unease that something isn't quite right. And they usually mask it with alcohol, or food, or drugs, or unfulfilling relationships or TV box sets.

But in truth, we are all guilty of this a little. The question is, how much time are we going to allow ourselves to be on autopilot? No one, not even a meditation master, remains in full control of their thoughts and actions all day long. It would be exhausting. But having the ability to be more aware, to be more mindful, and to question whether something is going to serve you or not, starts with knowing where you want to go — knowing where you want to go means that you can start saying no to the things that are not going to help you reach your goals.

So stop now and start writing about your best year. Be as descriptive as you need to be to feel excited. Own this process, make it work for you.

What Is Your Why?

In the next section, you will explore why you want the goals that you identified earlier. Why is it essential that you get your finances in order? Why is it important that your children have a stable upbringing? Why is it vital that you find intimacy in a relationship again? Why do you need to get in better shape?

You could say, I want to see my children as much as possible. I want to see them every other weekend and a couple of nights during the week and speak to them on the phone freely. That's great, but why do you really want that? Is it for the significance? Is it because you strongly identify with being a father? Is it because your parents weren't there when you were a kid, and you want to be there for your kids? I don't know what it is, but I promise you it's more profound. You're reading this book for a reason. There is a deeper why than the superficial one you are thinking of right now.

When I did this, I wanted all my debt paid off. But when I thought about why I wanted this, it was because I didn't want to feel enslaved and have to do things that I didn't want to do just because I was scared. That was a much more powerful motivator to achieve my objective than wanting to pay off my debt.

My why to live in Cornwall was because I wanted to have a home with my children where we could have a 'normal' life, cooking and eating dinner together, rather than hanging out in hotel rooms. Especially as my children grew older, I wanted to be present when they needed me, not just accessible every other weekend. Creating this environment was my real motivation; moving to Cornwall was the vehicle to achieve this.

I did this exercise with a client recently, and one of his goals was to find a new house. His challenge was that he couldn't afford a property near to his family home, so he was considering a house share, ten doors down in the same street as his family home. He knew that shared accommodation wouldn't be an ideal environment for his children to spend the night, but he liked the idea of being so close.

When we dug deeper, he found that his why was not to make it easier to see his children. It was to remain in the family home where he had spent the last 18 years. He had not yet made the mental shift that he was getting divorced and his situation was changing. He decided to ignore his situation and stay in the family home for as long as possible.

Once he was able to come to terms with his situation, he was able to think in more practical terms, moving a bus ride away to a more affordable area where he could have his own space and space for his children to stay. He also discovered that he wanted to put his own stamp on his new home and surround himself with things that interested him.

Once he found his reason why - to find a suitable environment for his children to stay where he could put his decorative stamp - he began to think of his goal, finding a house, positively and this motivated him to take action.

Now it's your turn. Write down why you want to achieve your goals. Get out of your head and write from your heart and ask yourself, why do I really want them? Why are these goals important to me? What will I feel when I've achieved them?

If you are still with me, well done. If you haven't done it, stop reading now and go back. Go on, do it you won't regret it. Have you done it? Great, let us continue.

How To Achieve Your Goals

You know where you currently are, you know what you want, and you know why you want it. This final section identifies the capabilities needed to get there. This is the 'how' and it is where you anchor in the actions that you need to take.

Your capabilities have got you this far. To reach your goals you need new capabilities, next-level capabilities. So, let's take a look at those goals and how you can achieve them.

Maybe one of your goals, is to find a new house for you and your children. To achieve this goal you will have to complete a number of steps, some of which may need to be broken down into further steps.

The first and most important step is to work out how much you can afford. Your personal circumstance will determine the tasks you need to take. It could be that you know to the penny, how much you have coming in each month and how much you spend. If this is the case you will be able to quickly calculate how much you can spend on a property. Or maybe you don't know, and like in the example, you have to put a few hours aside to dig out all of your statements to work out your incomings and outgoings

Next, you need to know how much child maintenance you are likely to receive. Again you may already know this or maybe you don't even know where to start. If it's the latter, you have further decisions to make. You could use an online calculator, contact your local Citizens Advice Office or let a divorce coach work it out for you. Once you know your budget, you can then start searching for properties to view that fall within your budget and meet your requirements.

Current Status	One Year Goals
• Worried about where I'm going to live	• Find a nice home for me and my children
Why These Goals Are Important	Capabilities Needed to Achieve Goals

• So my children have a happy and stable upbringing and we have a home to create happy memories together	• Need to work out how much I can afford
	   o Go through my statements to calculate my incomings and outgoings
	   o Find out how to calculate the amount of child maintenance I should get
	• Go on rightmove and search for property in my budget that meets my criteria
	• Shortlist potential properties and contact estate agents for viewings

When I did this, I realised that I needed to find and implement methods to manage my time more effectively to fit in work, travel, seeing my children, writing my book, setting up my own business, and spending time with my friends.

I wanted to see my kids as much as possible, so I knew that I had to find a way of building a new type of relationship with their mum so that access was not restricted. I had to learn how to manage and diffuse conflict. And if I was going to be successful at this, I knew that I needed to find out how to manage my own emotions and communicate effectively. I needed to upskill in many areas, and these learnings became the basis for this and my other books.

Take out your pen one last time and list the capabilities you need to achieve your goals. You now have a road map of where you are, where you want to go, why you want to go there, and how you are going to get there. This is very powerful information that should make you feel very confident about your future.

I do this exercise every three to six months. After I've done it, I check back on my previous session, and I'm amazed by how much progress I make. It's all to do with focus, whatever you focus your mind on, you will achieve.

Some people find that this exercise works better when you are being guided through it one on one with a coach. The coach can help you pinpoint what is important to you by asking the right questions to achieve clarity. If you have struggled with this process and needed extra guidance or if you feel that you can get even more from it, you can schedule a zoom call here: https://calendly.com/james-brien/clarity.

Coping in a Crisis

"In the midst of every crisis, lies great opportunity."

Albert Einstein

A s of writing, an estimated 2.6 billion[1] or one-third of the world's population is living under some kind of lockdown or quarantine. Many of us feel, understandably, uneasy about the sudden, strange upheaval to regular life as we know it.

Bars and restaurants are closed, and holidays, sport and entertainment cancelled. Instead, we have social distancing measures, indefinite lockdown, panic buying and harmful rhetoric.

The full psychological impact will not be known until after the crisis, but studies from previous disasters give a good idea of what to expect.

---

[1] Buchholz, Kathharina, What Share of the World Population Is Already on COVID-19 Lockdown?, http://www.statista.com, April 2020

In late February 2020, The Lancet[2] published a review of 24 studies documenting the psychological impact of quarantine. The findings offer a glimpse of what is in store in hundreds of millions of households around the world.

In short, and perhaps unsurprisingly, people in quarantine are very likely to develop a wide range of psychological symptoms. These include low mood, insomnia, stress, anxiety, anger, irritability, emotional exhaustion, depression and post-traumatic stress disorder. The study notes that low mood and irritability stand out as being very common.

In China, these expected mental health effects have appeared in the first research papers about the lockdown.

Of course, it's natural to have worries or fears in this environment. There is a risk of infection, the fear of becoming sick or of losing loved ones, a temporary loss of freedom, as well as the prospect of financial hardship. If we then layer on the emotional stresses of separation and divorce, it's clear that we need to look after ourselves to hold off and reduce the psychological impact.

The good news is that life's toughest challenges can provide an opportunity to take a look at our lives and decide what matters most to us and what we really want.

Like you, I have struggled with several significant life changes over the years, and I got through them by focusing on what kept me emotionally stable and happy, despite external turbulence. What follows is what you can do to stay mentally and physically strong, not just through the COVID-19 crisis, but through any crisis, you may face.

---

[2] Brooks ... et al, The psychological impact of quarantine and how to reduce it: rapid review of the evidence

Keep a Daily Routine

To a lesser or greater extent, we all harbour a desire, to be truly free. That is, to do what we want, when we want, with no interference from a boss, colleagues or family members. Those working full time from home will have less freedom than those furloughed, or out of work, but lockdown can give you a taste of what this is like, and it can feel like a dream.

For those working, establishing a routine might be more manageable. For the last ten years, I've worked remotely - at home, in transit, and hot-desking at offices, and I've found the key to success is structure. I also know that if you don't create a routine, life can start to go into a downward spiral.

Establish a morning routine that includes getting up and preparing for the day as if you were going to the office, will get you ready mentally for a day of work, and it helps you separate work from your home life which is vital for balance.

One of the biggest benefits of working from home is the flexible hours, but you must define your working hours. Many people worry that working from home leads to less work, but from experience, the opposite is true. Without the discipline of working hours, you can find your day stretched from early morning into the evening.

Once you've defined your schedule, share it with your boss and colleagues to set boundaries and manage expectations. If you don't do this already, now is the time to start switching off email and only dealing with it during set times. This simple hack reduces distractions and improves productivity.

Keeping your home organised, predictable and clean, counters all the uncertainly happening outside your home.

Studies[3] have shown that chronic clutter can leave your body constantly in a low-level fight-or-flight mode, which is taxing on your body and mind.

If you want to have a structured day, you need a place to work. Set aside a spot as your work area, choosing a location that will help you focus and avoid distractions. I recommend a room that has plenty of light to keep you energised.

For those not working, take this extra time at home as an opportunity to make yourself more marketable. Perhaps now is the time to seriously look at starting a new business or transition into another career. Read a book or take an online course (many are currently free) to cope with the uncertainty that lies ahead. More information on improving your finances and career potential, and starting your own business can be found in my next book. Sign up for special pre-release access at www.themindfuldivorcebook.com.

Stay Connected

Healthy relationships are essential for our well-being. Studies at Harvard[4] (Mineo, 2017) found that close personal connections are vital for our happiness and longevity throughout life. Engaging with other people boosts our immune system, and makes it less likely that we experience stress, anxiety and depression.

It is for this reason that one of the most important things you can do when going through divorce or separation or any trauma is to connect with and get support from friends. Sometimes this is more challenging for men than women as

---

[3] Darby E. Saxbe, Rena Repetti, No Place Like Home: Home Tours Correlate With Daily Patterns Of Mood and Coritsol, Personality and Social Psychology Bulletin, 2009, P71 - 81
[4] Mineo, Liz, Good genes are nice, but joy is better, The Harvard Gazette, 2017

often men do not keep in regular touch with their friends, but one of the benefits of the lockdown is that most people are at home, desperate to see a new face and talk with different friends.

It wasn't long ago that technology and social media were lambasted for increasing anxiety and depression and making us feel socially isolated. Now, most of us are using it to build a sense of real-life community. You can play online games together, and even have dinner dates using apps like Zoom.

Even Facebook, which has been experiencing a slow decline of users over the last few years has seen users flooding back to engage with friends and shared interest groups.

There are lots of opportunities to connect, so commit to speaking with at least one person every day. Just make sure that these people will uplift you and ditch those that will pull you down - you need to protect yourself as much as possible.

Lockdown affects us all differently. Some will find it easy, some extremely hard, and all of us will have good days and bad days. Don't hesitate to connect with a friend; you might find you are able to help them as well as yourself.

If you live with other people, keep in mind that we all deal with stress and react differently. If you find yourself getting irritated, take a few breaths before responding to someone else's behaviour to avoid reacting in a way that you later might regret. You may find that it is better to be honest and open about how you feel to foster understanding rather than potentially building resentment.

For more guidance on effective communication and diffusing conflict, look out for the second book in this series (get pre-release access at www.themindfuldivorcebook.com) or read chapter three in The Real Man's Guide to Divorce.

Reduce Negative Influences and Turn off That TV!

News stories are overwhelmingly about things we cannot influence. The daily repetition of news about things we can't act upon grinds us down and makes us feel fearful and helpless. News outlets do this to get your attention and keep you watching, but they are competing with everything else in your life, and so the only way to get your attention is to startle you, so that you focus on their message. The problem is that what we focus on, produces the emotions we feel, so if the news is about how disastrous everything is, that the world is ending, and we can never go back to normal again, we are going feel pretty awful.

So, we have to control our focus, and that isn't just during the COVID-19 crisis. In any day of your life, you can become completely depressed and overwhelmed. All you have to do is think about all of the people starving every single day. Or about all the injustice in the world or all of the people that have just died.

Or you can think about all the children who were just born, the acts of kindness that happen every single minute. The scientists who are working on solutions to the world's problems. What we focus on directly impacts our quality of life, so stop allowing negative influences into your life.

Instead feed your mind with something that will inspire you, or give you a new skill or philosophy of looking at life in a better way. In the appendix, I have recommended some books and podcasts to get you started.

Have fun doing things you enjoy like painting, baking, playing board games, dancing, speaking to friends who cheer you up, watching or reading something that makes you smile.

Think about what gave you pleasure as a child, and dedicate at least 30–60 minutes a day to activities that make you feel most happy and put a smile on your face. Laughter is known to make us feel better and can soothe physical tension, strengthen our immune system and give us pain relief.

Take a Break from Technology and Embrace Nature

Being at home means that many of us are spending more time than ever working, socialising, and entertaining ourselves through our devices. Studies have linked heavy smartphone use to stress, depression and anxiety, so it makes sense to give ourselves breaks from technology.

Simple hacks include making your bedroom a phone-free room; restricting usage between 9 am and 9 pm; turning off non-essential notifications, and deleting social media or other potentially time-wasting apps.

Counter the negative effects of technology by spending time in nature. Studies show that nature can have a positive impact on our health by lowering our blood pressure and boosting happiness.

Plan time in your garden, or take socially-distanced exercise in a nearby park. This will also give you a much-needed boost of Vitamin D, which is almost impossible to get enough from in food form and is essential for bone health and brain function.

Look After Your Health, Eat Well, Take Exercise and Sleep

The UK government recommends healthy adults engage in at least 2.5 hours of moderate exercise every week. Exercise is well known to stimulate the body to produce natural feel-good hormones which boost our perceived quality of life, make our problems seem more manageable and reduces anxiety and depression.

If you are already a regular gym-goer, you will find that many of the big chains provide online classes to do at home. Even if you are not a gym member, there are lots of paid classes on websites such as beachbodyondemand.com as well as free classes on YouTube and Instagram.

With restaurants and takeaways closed, more of us are eating healthy home-cooked food. Even if you have never cooked before, take this opportunity to learn and get in the kitchen and experiment.

Develop a regular relaxing bedtime routine such as a bath, a herbal tea and reading a book before bed. Make sure your bedroom is as quiet and dark as possible, and avoid looking at your phone an hour before bed as the blue light from the screens can affect sleep cycles.

Be Mindful and Open to Opportunity

As restrictive as the world may feel right now, think of the stay at home policy as an opportunity to refocus your attention from the external to the internal. Set your sights on long-avoided tasks, reorganise, or create something you've always wanted to. Approaching this time with a mindset of feeling trapped or stuck will only stress you out more. Instead of ruminating about being stuck inside, reframe your thoughts and be thankful for the opportunity to focus on yourself and your home.

Just a few minutes of meditation each day has been shown to have a multitude of positive effects on our mental and physical well-being, and now is a great time to start and establish a lifelong habit. Over the medium-term, research has shown that meditation can help calm down racing anxious minds; decrease stress and depressive feelings; open up new perspectives, and find inner stillness even when the outer world seems disorderly.

Being mindful is a term that gets thrown around a lot, but it simply means being non-judgmentally aware of the present moment, instead of drifting into thoughts about the past or the future. During difficult times it's easy for our attention to drift to worries about worst-case scenarios that may never happen. The fact is, no one knows what the future holds. It is prudent to be practically prepared, but after that, it is helpful to remember that we are safe in the present moment, rather than diving into negative thought spirals.

Acknowledge Your Feelings and Be Kind to Yourself

Human nature means that we are usually harsher on ourselves than we would be to anyone else. Some of the things we say to ourselves, we wouldn't dream of saying to our friends; in fact, in some cases we wouldn't have any friends left if we did, so learn to treat yourself like a best friend instead.

If you're not feeling as productive as usual, perhaps because you are juggling work and home-schooling, do what you can and accept that you're trying your best during an unprecedented, stressful situation. This could also be an opportunity to step back a little from your usual busy life and learn to forgive yourself if you are not feeling 100%, or if you fail to meet unrealistic standards.

Good advice at any time and especially now is not to compare yourself with other people's attitudes or achievements. We all handle things differently at different times and people only present the image they want you to see, so we never really know what someone else is going through.

Try to acknowledge uncomfortable feelings rather than stifle them. A good way to do this is to sit quietly with them and feel where they originate from in the body, making a mental note of what they are; I'm feeling anxious; I'm feeling bored; I'm feeling sad. Observing our feelings in such a way helps us recognise that we are not our feelings, that they come and go. And don't forget if you are feeling low, or worried about your feelings, reach out to friends for support.

Help Other People

Reaching out to others who might be feeling alone, anxious or overwhelmed can help us get through hard times together. Try and think of a person each day that you haven't spoken to for a while that might benefit from a message, call or supportive voice note. Helping others boosts our mental well-being like nothing else. We will do so much more for others than we will ever do for ourselves. When other people are counting on us, we can forget about our own problems as we focus our attention on helping them. Being in this problem solving frame of mind can give us a new perspective as well as the confidence to overcome our own challenges.

Food banks and family charities are in desperate need of support, and lots of opportunities are available to help the vulnerable in your area. Even if you are working, check in on your neighbours to see if they need any help collecting shopping or just to put a smile on their faces.

To Conclude

These are uncertain times where many of us face anxiety, financial pressure and loss of freedom, so it is imperative to look after our physical and mental well-being during this period.

We can do this by:

- Maintaining a routine
- Keeping regular connect with friends
- Minimising the consumption of negative content and feeding our minds with enjoyable experiences
- Regulating our use of technology and getting out in nature
- Looking after our bodies and minds by exercising, eating healthily and getting enough sleep
- Practising mindfulness and be kind to ourselves
- Helping others who are vulnerable, lonely or in need

By following these steps, we will not only survive and get through this period but come out the other side as improved beings, with a better understanding of ourselves and what is truly important to us.

What makes human beings happy is progress. And the progress doesn't even need to be huge. If you keep moving in the right direction, steady and consistent, you will get to wherever you want to go.

Summary

"It does not matter how slowly you go as long as you do not stop."

Confucius

The end of your relationship with your partner is going to be a painful, emotional period. Negative emotions are especially challenging to deal with because we tend to avoid talking about them. In the same way that there is a stigma about mental health issues, there is a stigma around expressing and talking about our feelings.

We are taught from a very early age to suppress our feelings, but feelings are useful. They tell us that we need to deal with something to move forward in life. Managing our stress levels helps us identify and respond to these signals appropriately, creating a virtuous circle of less stress, increased control and happiness.

Working out what went wrong helps us draw a line in the sand and put our mistakes behind us. It is this knowing of how we contributed to our breakup that gives us the confidence and sense of peace that powers us forward, perhaps into a new relationship.

We only have 1440 minutes at our disposal every day. How we choose to spend this time will define the quality of our lives. If we decide to be mainly joyful, we will have a wonderful life. If we choose to stay angry, we will be miserable.

Research has shown that four minutes of anger suppresses our immune system for four hours.[5] When we get angry with a person or situation, we are literally damaging ourselves. We reduce the effectiveness of our immune system and increase our risk of getting sick, all because of our anger.

The gratitude exercise is your secret weapon against all negative and damaging emotions. Use it daily and train your mind to focus on the good in your life, as our thoughts determine how we feel, our feelings govern our actions, and our actions deliver our quality of life.

In our busy world, we are constantly bombarded with messages designed to persuade us to think or act in a certain way. Often this leads us away from, not towards our goals. The clarity exercise not only helps us decide what we want from life, but it also reveals our why. Knowing why something is important to us, keeps us strong and focused even when life gets tough and tries to knock us from our path.

Lastly, we looked at how to cope during the greatest crisis of our time. All crises can provide us with opportunities, but we need to take action to hold off and reduce its psychological impact. By following the steps suggested, you will not only survive this period, but you will emerge from the other side as

---

[5] Glen Rein; Mike Atkinson; Rollin McCraty, Ph.D., The Physiological and Psychological Effects of Compassion and Anger, Journal of Advancement in Medicine. 1995, 8(2): 87-105

an improved being, with a better understanding of yourself and what is truly important to you.

After I published my first book, people began reaching out to me for advice. The question they all asked was if the stress and aggravation that they were experiencing would ever end. Some were so worn down by their circumstances that they couldn't see a way out, and it seemed to consume all elements of their life.

When life is beating us like this, we find it difficult to look to the future. But we must. Life ebbs and flows; it has ups and downs. We can't control what life throws at us, but we can control how we deal with our circumstances. This mindset is the central theme throughout this book, and I hope you will use it to your advantage. Doing so will have a profound effect, both during this challenging period and throughout the rest of your life.

If you follow the advice in this book and implement the advised methods, you will not only start to feel better, but you will also come through the process happier, more durable and healthier. Implementation, actually taking action, is the key, so to facilitate this, I have created a checklist below to keep you on track.

I sincerely wish you all the best, and I look forward to hearing your success stories. You can reach me at james@themindfuldivorcebook.com.

Checklist

- Manage stress levels by listing and prioritising everything that you must do. Only focus on what you can control. Creating the list will not only increase your productivity so that you can get through the tasks, but also reduce the chances of you becoming overwhelmed.

- Work out what went wrong, and think about how you contributed to the breakup. Apologise if you need to and then let go. The process allows you to close the door on the past, knowing that you will avoid the same mistakes in future relationships.

- Complete the values exercise to understand your motivations and what is important to you. Live your life congruent with your values.

- Focus on what you have, rather than what you don't have. The daily gratitude exercise helps you appreciate all of the positives in your life which will help raise your spirits and move you forward in your life.

- Decide what your life goals are. These should influence every decision you make, helping you make the right decisions for the long term and, more importantly, helping you avoid being knocked off track by outside influences.

Always take care of yourself, but pay particular attention to this during times of crisis. By following a few simple steps, you will emerge from any crisis healthier and happier.

If you have found this book helpful, please take a minute to leave a review on Amazon. This will help other people find the book.

Appendix

Recommended Reading List

- Byrne, Rhonda, The Secret, 2006
- Carnegie, Dale, How to Win Friends and Influence People, 2006
- Ferriss, Timothy The 4-Hour Work Week, 2008
- Frankl, Viktor E, Man's Search for Meaning, 2004
- Robbins, Anthony, Unlimited Power, 2001

Recommended Podcasts

- Ten Percent Happier with Dan Harris
- The Dean Graziosi Show
- The Tony Robbins Podcast
- Happier Podcast with Gretchen Rubin

Recommended Website

If you live in England or Wales and your partner agrees to a divorce, visit www.easyonlinedivorce.co.uk for a fast and easy divorce. The application takes minutes, and you will save thousands on legal fees compared to high street solicitors.

Acknowledgements

Thanks to Tony Robbins, Dean Graziosi and the KBB family for inspiring me to work hard every day to help more people.

Thank you to my editor, Nicola Cassidy, for her valuable feedback and her ability to help me to get my message clear, and to Natalie Rimmer for creating another beautiful cover design.

Finally, I want to give a big thanks to my friends that have kept me sane during the lockdown. The phone calls, aperitif's over zoom and virtual pub quizzes have been a lifeline over this challenging time. It has made me re-remember how important friendships are.